westlife

the official poster book and factfile

EDDIE ROWLEY

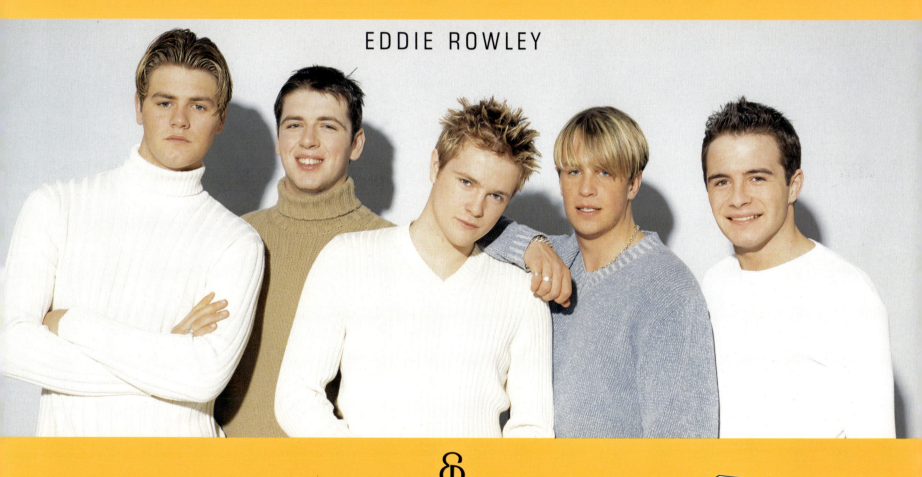

EBURY PRESS

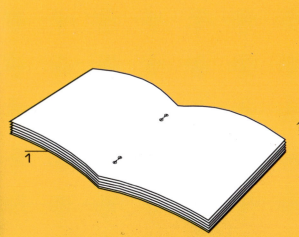

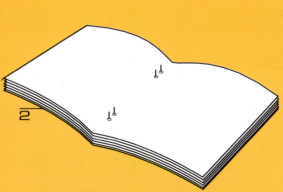

To make the most of your Official WESTLIFE Poster Book, open the book to the middle pages and lie it on a flat surface.

Next, using a blunt knife, carefully prise open the staples so that the staple-ends point straight up into the air.

Then, simply "lift" the posters away from the staples.

message to our
fans

We want to say a big, huge thank you to all our fans. It's you who have put us where we are today. In Ireland, our fans gave us huge support and now that has spread around the world. It's amazing to look back and see how far we've come and to see the fan base growing. All of us are genuine lads and we see you, the fans, as people. We don't just take you for granted. No matter where we are or what country we're in, we try to stop and speak to you and spend as much time as possible with you. If you stick with us for the future, we'll be there for you. No matter what country you're in, we'll always come back. Let's have some great times together.

Love from Westlife.

Shane Filan

Brian McFadden

Nicky Byrne

Kian "Noise" Egan

MARK FEEHILY

kian
factfile

PLACE OF BIRTH: Sligo, Ireland

DATE OF BIRTH: 29 April, 1980

STARSIGN: Taurus

HEIGHT: 1.75m

COLOUR OF EYES: Blue

COLOUR OF HAIR: Blond

IDENTIFYING FEATURE: Small scar on his face

PARENTS: Kevin and Patricia

BROTHERS: Tom, Gavin and Colm

SISTERS: Vivienne, Marielle and Fenella

GIRLFRIEND: None

BEST SCHOOL SUBJECTS: Art, Music and Building Construction

HOBBIES: Working out in the gym, music and shopping

"Babe magnet" is a term that applies to Kian Egan. With his blond locks, piercing blue eyes and cheeky grin, Kian has launched a million female dreams.

The hunk with the fun-loving personality admits he's savouring every glorious moment as he careers through the wacky world of pop.

Kian's feet haven't touched the ground since Westlife was launched to superstardom. "It's been a real buzz," he enthuses. "Having girls screaming at you wherever you go is just the best feeling in the world. I'm the luckiest guy alive right now."

But the country boy with the easy-going attitude is determined that life in the fast lane is not going to change him.

He says: "We've learned a lot about dealing with stardom from Boyzone and from our co-manager Ronan Keating. They taught us that you can have major success and still stay 'normal'.

"I don't think there's any chance of me becoming big-headed about Westlife's achievements, because my family are there to keep my feet on the ground. They would call me a sap if I started playing the star at home. My mam would give me a clip around the ears."

Kian is proud of the fact that his mother is one of his biggest supporters. "She even goes to church and prays for me and Westlife," he says. "She's forever lighting candles so that the band will do well and to keep us safe on our travels around the world."

Kian admits he would love to find someone special to share his life, but being in a busy pop band doesn't leave much time for love.

"It can get lonely and it would be nice to have a girlfriend, but it's just not possible right now," he admits.

"We don't lead the type of lifestyle that would suit marriage and kids. We'll be working hard, flying around the world for at least the next five years.

"I'm not complaining though because it's a long life. I'm only 19 and there will be lots of time for love when I've built up my career."

He doesn't rule out the possibility of dating a fan. "You never know who you're going to fall in love with, so you can't make rules," he says. "If the right person comes along and she happens to be a fan, you can't deny that love. I would embrace it whether she was a fan or not."

DESERT ISLAND DILEMMA

KIAN ON HIS DREAM HOME:

Who would you like to be stranded on a desert island with? Cameron Diaz because she has beautiful eyes.

KIAN ON WESTLIFE:

westlife
kian

nicky factfile

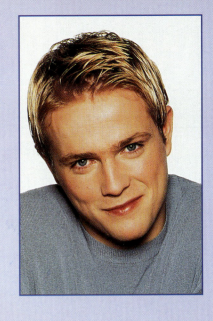

PLACE OF BIRTH: Dublin, Ireland

DATE OF BIRTH: 9 October, 1978

STARSIGN: Libra

HEIGHT: 1.75m

COLOUR OF EYES: Blue

COLOUR OF HAIR: blond

IDENTIFYING FEATURE: Scar on right elbow

PARENTS: Nikki and Yvonne

BROTHER: Adam

SISTER: Gillian

GIRLFRIEND: Georgina Ahern

BEST SCHOOL SUBJECTS: English, Geography and PE

HOBBIES: Flying and travelling

NICKY ON WESTLIFE'S SONG:

"Ronan Keating says he'd

Nicky is regarded as the gentleman of the group, the Ronan-type figure who is always looking after the interests of the other guys.

It's not surprising to discover that Ronan Keating is his hero and Nicky can't believe that he's now working with his idol.

He says: "I always admired Ronan and I copied him and he was my role model in pop. When I got the chance to work with him, it was unbelievable. I was star-struck at first, but he's so down-to-earth that he soon made me feel comfortable.

"He's just brilliant in every way. He's a great manager and a great friend. He invited the whole band out to dinner in his house at the start. You'd die for his house, it's unbelievable. Himself and his wife Yvonne are the nicest couple in the world."

Nicky grew up listening to Bros and A-Ha, his older sister's favourite groups. "I loved their singing and I used to constantly listen to their albums," he reveals.

Nicky's dad had a band called Nikki and The Studs and as a kid Nicky Jnr used to help them set up the gear and then watch them perform. It was his education in the music business.

He says: "The first time I was ever on stage was at my auntie's wedding and I sang Karma Chameleon by Boy George. After that experience, I was hooked."

Initially, Nicky pursued a career in soccer and landed a place with the Leeds United youths team as a goalie.

He says: "When I went to Leeds, I was constantly singing and all the lads used to say I should be in Boyzone rather than a footballer. In the end, I didn't grow tall enough to be a goalkeeper, but as I headed back to Dublin I was really excited about my plans to set up a boy band. I really wanted Louis Walsh to be involved and I can't believe how well it all worked out for me."

Nicky is the only member of Westlife who has a girlfriend. He's dating Georgina Ahern, the eldest daughter of Taoiseach Bertie Ahern, the Irish Prime Minister.

He says: "Georgina is beautiful and placid and my soul mate. She's so perfect for me. I'm also lucky to get on well with her Dad, as we both share an interest in sport.

"The fans have been especially good to both myself and Georgina. Having a girlfriend starting off in a boy band isn't very cool, but our brilliant fans accepted it so well.

"They even gave Georgina Christmas presents last year, as they did to all of us. When they meet Georgina in Dublin, they always stop and talk to her. I'm really lucky to have such wonderful, loyal followers."

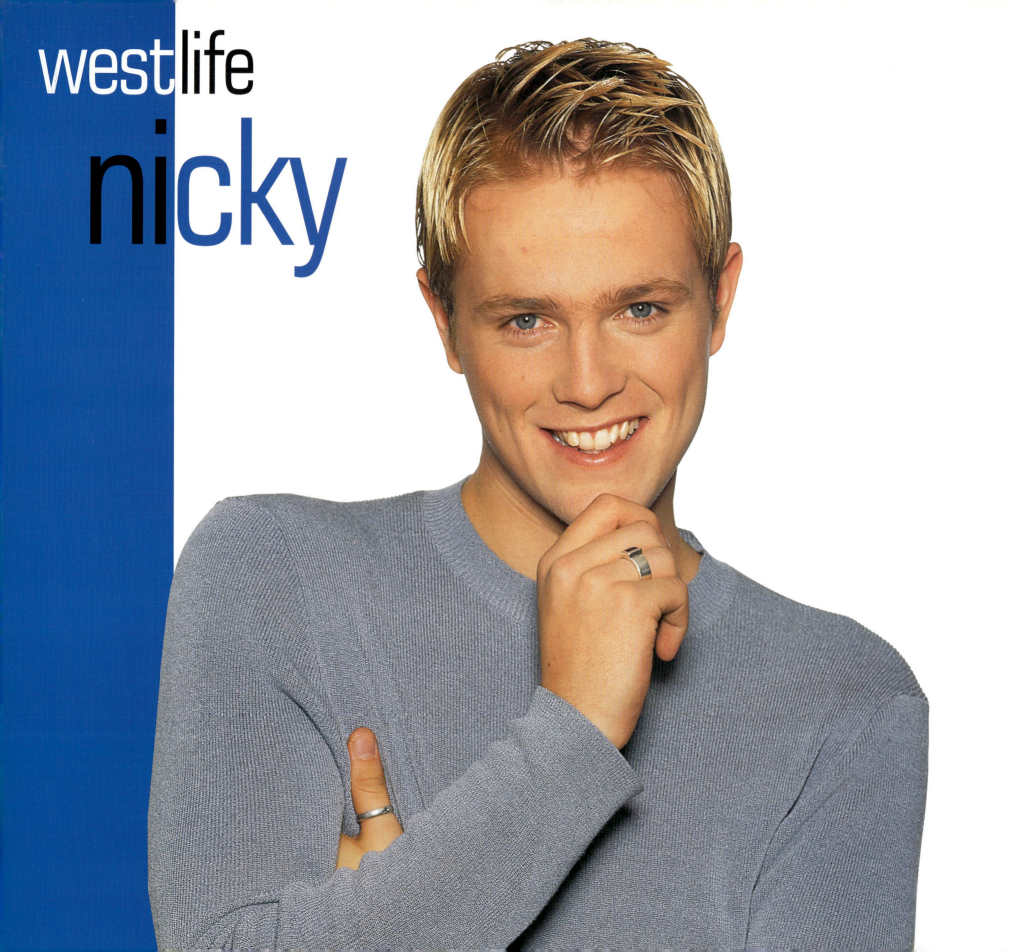

westlife
nicky

shane
factfile

PLACE OF BIRTH: Sligo, Ireland

DATE OF BIRTH: 5 July, 1979

STARSIGN: Cancer

HEIGHT: 1.75m

COLOUR OF EYES: Hazel green

COLOUR OF HAIR: Dark brown

IDENTIFYING FEATURE: None

PARENTS: Peter and Mae

BROTHERS: Finbar and Liam

SISTERS: Yvonne, Denise and Mairead

GIRLFRIEND: None

BEST SCHOOL SUBJECTS: English and Accountancy

HOBBIES: Horse riding

Shane Filan conveys the image of being reserved and serious, but behind his mature exterior lurks a wild, fun-fuelled animal.

While he adopts a serious approach to his work in Westlife, Shane also knows how to switch off and enjoy himself along with the other members of the group.

He does admit that he was regarded as "a messer" by his teachers during his school days. "I was always in trouble for not paying attention and I still have a low attention span," he reveals.

One of the first things he had to learn when he became a pop star was how to cope with a lifestyle that involved flying around the world.

He says: "It was the only real downside of my amazing career when I first started off, as I hated flying. I just didn't know how I was going to cope with the boredom of being stuck on a plane for hours.

"I always considered the flight from Dublin to London a long one. I thought it would never end and that just takes an hour. Imagine then how I felt when I learned that we were going to faraway places like Australia and Taiwan, which takes over twenty hours!

"But, like everything else, the more you do it, the more you get used to it. Now it's like getting on a bus and just as well too – it looks like I'm going to be spending the next five to ten years on a plane!"

One of the best things about being in WestLife for Shane is the fact that he gets to indulge his passion for shopping. He's a confessed shopaholic.

He says: "Nicky, Kian and myself are the shoppers in the group. We've been doing a bit of that, but I'm looking forward to really going at it when the money comes in and we get some time off."

While he has already been around the world and seen some exotic places, Shane admits that the most magical place on earth to him is still his native Sligo.

He would love to eventually build a mansion there and live in that picturesque area of Ireland with the woman of his dreams.

Shane says: "I am already designing the house in my mind. It will have dark brick on the outside, wooden floors on the inside and lots of things that I will pick up on my travels in the years ahead."

SHANE ON RELIGION:

"Praying is big in my family. We pray every night."

DESERT ISLAND DILEMMA

Who would you like to be stranded on a desert island with?

SHANE ON WHAT HE'S GOING

bryan factfile

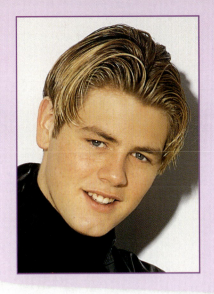

PLACE OF BIRTH: Dublin, Ireland

DATE OF BIRTH: 12 April, 1980

STARSIGN: Aries

HEIGHT: 1.86m

COLOUR OF EYES: Blue

COLOUR OF HAIR: Blond

IDENTIFYING FEATURE: Birthmark on lower back

PARENTS: Brendan and Mairead

SISTER: Susan

GIRLFRIEND: None

BEST SCHOOL SUBJECTS: Science, Maths and English

HOBBIES: None

DESERT ISLAND DILEMMA

Who would you like to be stranded on a desert island with? Jennifer Lopez for obvious reasons. Darina Allen (Irish chef) to cook the food while I'm on the

Bryan McFadden, the taller of Westlife's three blond bombshells, is the cheeky one in the group.

He's always pulling pranks on the other guys and is definitely the joker in the pack. The rest of his Westlife mates regard him as the Robbie "Wild Man" Williams of the band.

Bryan enjoys having a laugh. "I know how to wind people up and it's one way of passing the time when we're hanging around waiting for things to happen," he says.

"I think it's important to hold on to your sense of humour because there are lots of times when you really need it in this business. Even though it's a great life, there are times when the pressure gets too much. Being a bit silly gets you through it. I make the other guys laugh."

One of the best things about being in Westlife for Bryan is all the female attention he enjoys.

But he still can't believe the frenzied buzz the band generates among girls when they appear in public.

"One day when we were doing a TV show in the UK, loads of girls turned up to see us and some of them fainted! I was amazed that us lads had that effect on them," Bryan says.

"Even though so much has happened for us this year, we still think of ourselves as just ordinary guys. It's true that we're not doing an ordinary job because this is a mad, mad life we lead, but we're still just five normal lads from Dublin and Sligo. Prick us and we bleed like everyone else."

"We'll always stay that way and every now and then we have a group meeting just to make sure that everyone is staying grounded and that no one has any problems."

While his poster now adorns the walls of besotted teenage girls, Bryan admits that he was "a fat kid with no friends" during his early school days. "It was a terrible time," he says.

Bryan admits he's still overwhelmed by his rapid rise to pop stardom. "I never thought I'd make it this far in the pop business and it was a shaky time at the start," he reveals.

"I didn't know until the final hour that I was going to be in the line-up, so it was scary and a huge relief when I got the good news.

"Every day since then has been a brilliant one for me. I nearly have to pinch myself to believe it.

"The only real downside is having to get up very early in the morning, particularly as we have late nights. But it still beats having to get up for school or work on a Monday morning.

"Being in Westlife is a better education than any college. We're getting to see the world and all the different cultures. You couldn't learn that kind of stuff out of a book. And we're getting paid to do it!"

mark factfile

PLACE OF BIRTH: Sligo, Ireland

DATE OF BIRTH: 28 May, 1980

STARSIGN: Gemini

HEIGHT: 1.78m

COLOUR OF EYES: Blue

COLOUR OF HAIR: Light brown

IDENTIFYING FEATURE: None

PARENTS: Oliver and Marie

BROTHERS: Barry (14) and Colin (9)

SISTERS: None

GIRLFRIEND: None, but open to offers

BEST SCHOOL SUBJECTS: Home Economics, English and PE

HOBBIES: Tennis, badminton and squash

Tall, dark and handsome, Mark Feehily is the quiet and serious one in the group.

He is like everyone else's big brother. Although he's mild mannered and reserved, when he does speak the others all listen because they regard him as being wise and respect his views.

Although he now has girls chanting his name outside hotels, TV studios and concert venues, Mark still doesn't regard himself as a star.

He says: "People like Celine Dion and Michael Jackson are stars. I have a long way to go in Westlife before I could come close to their kind of stardom and even then I don't think I'll feel any different to the person who grew up in the Irish countryside.

"I think people thought success would go to our heads, but we're all still the same down-to-earth lads who first auditioned for Westlife and we won't change."

While he is taking the phenomenal success of Westlife in his stride, Mark is genuinely thrilled to be a major part of the pop business today.

He says: "Two years ago nobody knew who I was, now I go to foreign countries and people shout my name. I go to parties and I see people like Robbie Williams and The Spice Girls. I'm not fazed by it all, but I do think it's pretty amazing that I'm a part of this world now."

It's been the realisation of a childhood fantasy for gentle giant Mark. "Things like appearing on TOP OF THE POPS was one of my dreams all my life," he says.

"I know how lucky I am. So many people never get a break, but mine has come right at the start of my working life. I'm doing something I love, so it means I'll never really work a day, because when you're doing something you love it's never work."

Mark has no one special in his life and he does admit that he was lonely when he first left home and set off around the globe with Westlife.

He says: "Nothing can prepare you for the initial pangs of loneliness you experience. Like everything else, it just takes time to get used to it. And I am used to it now. I've grown to accept that I won't see my family and friends for long periods at a time.

"It was great having Ronan Keating as our co-manager, because he's been through it all with Boyzone. He told us what it would be like, so we knew it wasn't just us who had those early problems to deal with. Ronan was always at the other end of a phone line and he's been very generous with his support and advice."

MARK ON BEING AWAY FROM HOME:

"Of all the lads, I probably miss home the most. Sometimes I sit in

MARK ON THE FUTURE OF WESTLIFE:

DESERT ISLAND DILEMMA

Who would you like to be stranded on a desert island with?
Mariah Carey

west life
mark

westlife
factfile

WHERE WAS THE GROUP FORMED?

It started out as a local pop band called I.O.U in Sligo, Ireland.

HOW DID IT START?

The original members were performing in a local production of the musical GREASE in December 1996. They were playing The T-birds. Later they were singing a Boyz II Men song, I Make Love To You, at an after-show party and someone suggested that they should form a group. They waited until they finished their school exams in the summer of '97 and the band was formed on 3 July of that year.

HOW DID THEY GET THEIR BIG BREAK?

Shane Filan's mum contacted Boyzone's manager Louis Walsh and asked him to check them out. Louis had already seen them when they made a brief appearance on Irish TV. Kian Egan and Shane Filan travelled to Dublin to meet Louis in February 1998 and he was impressed with them. He immediately got them a support spot to The Backstreet Boys in Dublin on 16 and 17 March. They went from playing to 100 people in their home town to 10,000 with The Backstreet Boys.

WHAT IS THE DIFFERENCE BETWEEN I.O.U. AND WESTLIFE?

A big difference. Louis held auditions in June 1998 and changed the line-up. Kian Egan, Shane Filan and Mark Feehily are the only original members remaining. They have been joined by Nicky Byrne and Bryan McFadden from Dublin.

HOW DID RONAN KEATING BECOME INVOLVED?

Louis asked Ronan to help him develop Westlife. When Ronan first saw them he couldn't believe their raw vocal talents, along with their great personalities and natural charm. He felt they had the potential to go far and he decided to give them the benefit of his experience in Boyzone.

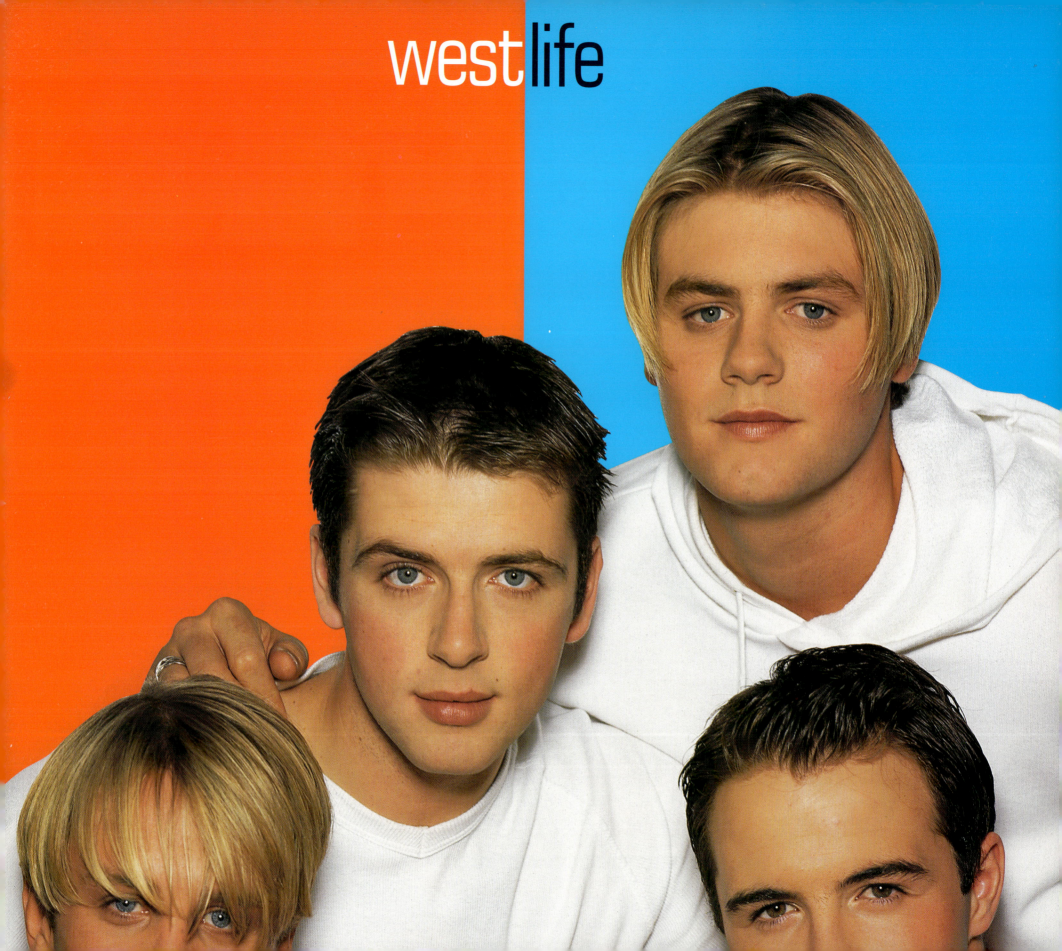

Yes and no. At least one major record company turned them down, but there was huge interest from the others. Louis and Ronan opted for a deal with RCA because of their phenomenal success with Take That and Five. WestLife was signed up by RCA in October 1998 and the champagne corks popped.

WHAT WAS THEIR INITIAL SUCCESS?

Their big break was joining the Smash Hits Roadshow and winning Best New Tour Act in December, 1998, an award that Boyzone had themselves won back in 1994. It was a sign of things to come.

HOW HAS RONAN HELPED THEM TO DEVELOP?

He gave them the support slot on Boyzone's tour and slipped out in disguise every night to watch them perform. Then he went to their dressing room after each performance to give them advice on how to improve their stage act.

WHAT OTHER BACK-UP DO THEY HAVE?

Westlife are working with the top producers in the music world today. They were also styled by Kenny Ho, the guru who created the winning images for The Spice Girls.

WHAT WAS THEIR INITIAL CHART SUCCESS?

When their first single, Swear It Again, was launched in Ireland in March 1999, it became the biggest selling debut single in the history of Irish pop, spending five weeks at Number One. It shot straight to the top spot in the UK pop charts when it was released in April and held that position for two weeks.

With success following around Europe, Asia, Australia and New Zealand, Westlife had emerged as the biggest and most exciting new pop act to hit the scene.

friends, but at least I have my mobile to keep in contact."

bigger than The Beatles."

Liam Gallagher. I met him this summer and he was rude to me

What three personal items would you take with you?
Mobile phone, my Discman and CDs and a bottle and note pad so that I can send a message in a bottle

What personal comfort would you miss?
My Mum's cooking

What song would you sing to help you cope?
I Wish That I Could Fly (Lenny Kravitz)

MARK ON HIS MOST EMBARRASSING MOMENT:

"I forgot the words to my song during a talent contest in front of one thousand people at the age of fourteen!"

20 THINGS TO KNOW ABOUT MARK

He describes himself as "shy, reserved, but also friendly"

Purple is his favourite colour

He has a pet dog called Snoopy

His ideal woman should be "thoughtful and funny"

He describes "singing all the time" as his bad habit

He once did pizza delivery and worked as a photo lab assistant

His previous band was I.O.U.

He plays piano, guitar and tin whistle

The first record he bought was Uptown Girl by Billy Joel

The first concert he attended was Michael Jackson in Dublin

ARMAGEDDON is his favourite film

His favourite actor is Eddie Murphy

Phoebe from FRIENDS is his favourite actress

THE WITCHES by Roald Dahl is his favourite book

Timberland is his favourite designer

He dislikes "narrow-minded people"

His favourite method of relaxation is "chilling out with my pals"

His favourite dish is chicken

He dislikes fish

One of his ambitions is to meet his idols Mariah Carey and Michael Jackson

MARK ON HIS FIRST VISIT TO AUSTRALIA:

"We ended up smack, bang in the city that HOME AND AWAY is made in. I'm a big fan and we wanted to visit the set but didn't have time. I never imagined that I would get to Australia."

MARK ON FLYING:

"I always take loads of CDs with me on long flights. It's a great way to listen to new music and it passes the time."

bryan
westlife

swimming away from the island!

Who would you not like to be stranded on a desert island with?
The band Five because there would be ten of us and that's too many young blokes on the island.

What three personal items would you take with you?
A mobile phone, CD walkman and a poster of Jennifer Lopez

What personal comfort would you miss?
A comfortable bed with a big, fat pillow

What song would you sing to help you cope?
Flying Without Wings (Westlife)

20 THINGS TO KNOW ABOUT BRYAN

He's always full of energy, even first thing in the morning

He has a passion for Britney Spears, but his ideal woman is also Jennifer Lopez

He describes himself as "fun and shy"

He'd love to have a girlfriend, but doesn't stop still enough to find one

His worst habit is forgetfulness

His favourite colour is red

His heroes are his Mum and Dad

He once worked in a bingo hall as a "caller" and was on the security staff at a McDonald's restaurant in Dublin

He gained experience as a performer with The Cartel Showband from Dublin

He plays guitar and piano

His favourite item of clothing is a baggy tracksuit

Dolce & Gabbana is his favourite designer gear

He loves Japanese food

His favourite film is TITANIC

Soccer is his favourite sport

His favourite book is THE GENERAL, about an Irish gangster

Leonardo DiCaprio is his favourite actor

The first concert he attended was Kylie Minogue in Dublin

The first record he bought was I Should Be So Lucky by Kylie Minogue

His favourite song is Something Stupid by Frank Sinatra

WESTLIFE MATES:

"We're best friends. When we're not working we're on the phone to each other all the time. I'll arrange to meet Nicky in Dublin and the other lads meet up in Sligo. I'm glad we get on so well. It would be hell travelling with people you didn't like."

"I'm wrecked, but I'm enjoying it. This time last year I was working in McDonalds in Artane (Dublin). Look at me now, I'm flying all over the world, so I'm not going to complain."

BRYAN ON MEETING THE STARS:

"I've got to meet lots of famous people since I joined Westlife and one of them was Mr Blobby. I got quite excited when I saw him because I grew up with him on the telly."

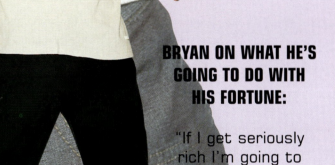

BRYAN ON WHAT HE'S GOING TO DO WITH HIS FORTUNE:

"If I get seriously rich I'm going to buy a Ferrari."

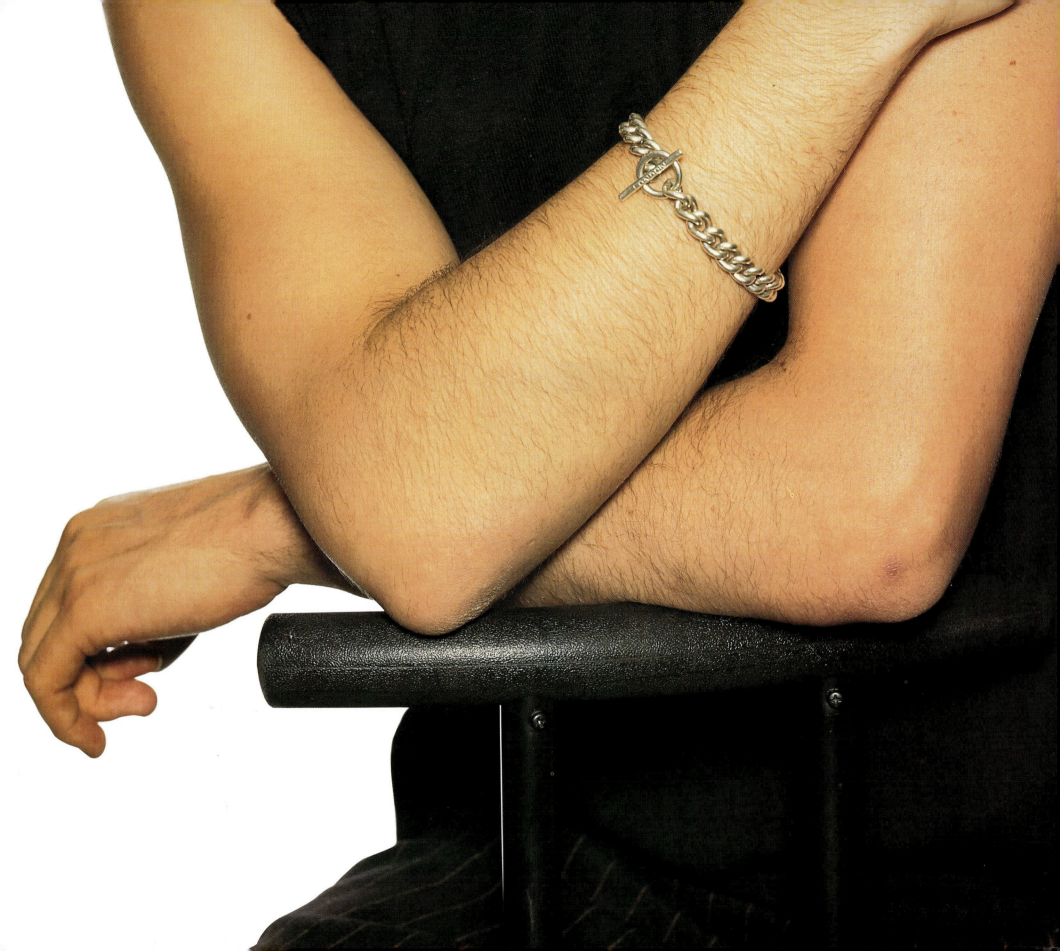

I bought a BMW last October, but I haven't had the chance to drive it since. Nicky sold his because he wasn't getting much use out of it, but at least my dad is driving mine!"

Bart Simpson

What three personal items would you take with you?
Mobile phone, a clock and food

What personal comfort would you miss?
My couch

What song would you sing to help you cope?
Always Look On The Bright Side Of Life

SHANE ON HIS CHILDHOOD PRANKS:

"I got into an awful lot of trouble one time when I broke FOUR of my neighbours' windows. But I learned a good lesson as I had to pay for the damage."

SHANE ON FAME:

"I worry about getting so famous that I have to go out in disguise to escape the paparazzi. I would hate to have them camped outside my door, that would be horrible."

SHANE ON LOOKS:

"While good looks do initially attract you to people, they're not all important at the end of the day. It's the person behind the looks that's important. Some people have plastic surgery and I can't understand why they do that."

20 THINGS TO KNOW ABOUT SHANE

He describes himself as "level-headed, generous, romantic"

He likes "sleeping, hot weather, girls"

He dislikes "rude people, rain, snakes"

His favourite food is Mum's cooking and steak and chips

"Anything by W.B. Yeats" are his favourite read

His ideal woman would be "cute and cuddly and one who loves me"

His favourite actress is Catherine Zeta Jones

Tom Cruise is his favourite actor

TITANIC is his favourite movie

His music/singing hero is Michael Jackson

One of his early jobs was working in a hardware store

His previous band was I.O.U.

He plays guitar

His favourite clothes are long sleeved shirts

Dolce & Gabbana is his favourite designer

The first record he bought was Billy Joel's Uptown Girl

His favourite song is Back For Good by Take That

The first concert he attended was Status Quo in Sligo

The pop performer he would most like to meet is Michael Jackson

If he was an animal he would like to be "a stallion"

He describes himself as "thoughtful, reliable and trustworthy"

His ideal woman is "elegant, smart and humorous with nice eyes"

His favourite colours are blue and white

He likes shopping and good restaurants

His favourite clothes are "smart clothes"

Gucci is his favourite designer

His worst habit is "drinking tea with the spoon still in the cup"

His heroes are Ronan Keating and Bruce Willis

He was a trainee goalkeeper at Leeds United

His most embarrassing moment was "falling over in front of 30,000 people at Elland Road (Leeds United's stadium)"

He is learning to play the piano

Soccer is his favourite sport

His favourite film is ARMAGEDDON

Brad Pitt and Bruce Willis are his favourite actors

Cameron Diaz is his favourite actress

His favourite song is Against All Odds by Phil Collins

His favourite food is "Mum's cooking and Japanese"

He dislikes "smoking and arrogant people"

The first concert he attended was The Cranberries in Dublin

The stars he would most like to meet are Phil Collins and Madonna

NICKY ON FLYING:

"I'm not scared of flying, but I always say a prayer before the plane takes off, just in case..."

EMBARRASSING MOMENT:

"It was my first performance with Westlife in front of 20,000 fans in Ballina, Ireland. I went on stage and forgot all the dance moves and words because I was just so overwhelmed."

NICKY ON BEING TURNED DOWN BY HIS GIRLFRIEND GEORGINA:

"When I first asked her out she said no. A year later, one of my mates asked her to go out with me and she said yes!"

NICKY ON THE FIRST TIME HE MET HIS GIRLFRIEND'S DAD:

"I was a nervous wreck. I was so shy I wasn't able to say more than 'Yes' and 'No' to his questions." After all, it was the then Minister For Finance sitting in front of me."

DESERT ISLAND DILEMMA

Who would you like to be stranded on a desert island with?
Georgina, my girlfriend. She'd kill me if I said anyone else!

Who would you not like to be stranded on a desert island with?
Anybody who's grumpy

What three personal items would you take with you?
A mobile phone with an unlimited battery, a radio and a speedboat

What personal comfort would you miss?
Sitting in my own front room having a cup of tea

What song would you sing to help you cope?
Flying Without Wings (Westlife)

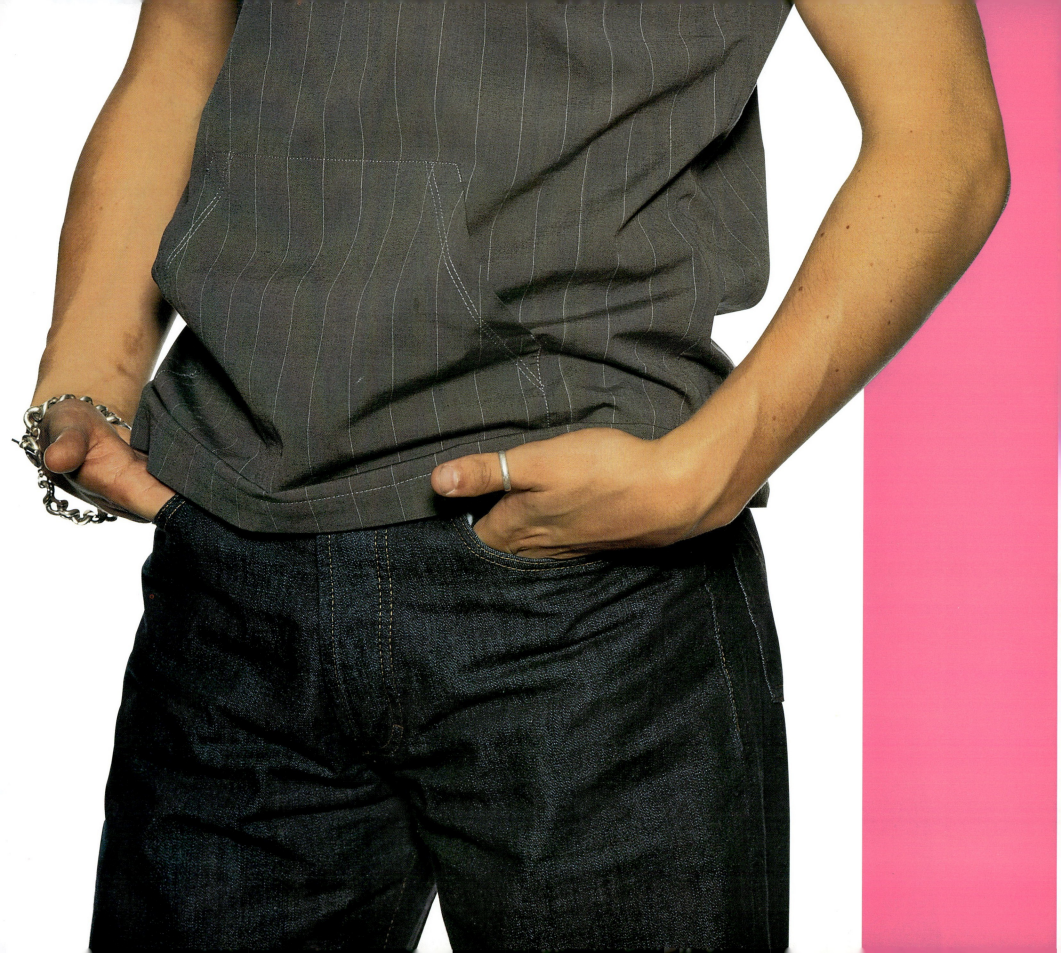

It would also have a special music room with a grand piano as the centre piece and lots of guitars and musical instruments everywhere. That would be MY room."

KIAN ON FANS:

"I love meeting them. I love doing signings because it gives me the chance to say thank you to all the people who put me where I am today."

KIAN ON HIS DAYS AS A KISSAGRAM:

"It was harmless fun. I used to wear a sequinned trousers and a dicky bow, nothing else. Going in to a hen party and reciting a poem dressed in that outfit took a lot of nerve, so it gave me the confidence to go on stage and was all part of my training for Westlife."

Margaret Thatcher

What three personal items would you take with you?
Mobile phone, CD player and Cameron Diaz poster

What personal comfort would you miss?
My bed

What song would you sing to help you cope?
She's Like The Wind

on to excite the girls. We want our music to get inside them and make them feel happier about themselves."

KIAN ON HIS DAYS AS A MOONIE:

"When I was younger, I used to play football and on the bus journey I often flashed my bare bum out the back window for a laugh."

20 THINGS TO KNOW ABOUT KIAN

He's moody when he wakes up in the morning

He describes himself as "romantic, fun and shy"

His worst habit is biting his nails

His favourite food is steak and chips

He likes a girl with good looks, but she should have a fun personality

He plays guitar and piano

The first record he bought was by the heavy metal group Metallica

The first concert he attended was Michael Jackson in Dublin

His favourite song of all time is She's Like The Wind (from DIRTY DANCING)

His favourite colour is white

His favourite designer is Dolce & Gabbana

His favourite casual clothes are a white Alexander McQueen shirt and Nicole Farhi cotton jeans

His early part-time job was working as an assistant in a clothes shop

He played in three local rock bands before pop stardom came along

His favourite actor is Brad Pitt

Cameron Diaz is his favourite actress

His favourite book is BRAVO 2 ZERO (Andy McNabb)

He dislikes bad manners in a person

The animal he would most like to be is a lion

His ambition is to meet his hero Michael Jackson

westlife

Westlife got a real taste of superstardom when they hit Asia during the summer and were mobbed by frenzied fans.

Kian Egan says: "The fans are crazy there. As soon as you emerge from a building they jump on you. They just want a piece of you. I had a ring pulled off my hand and Nicky had a crucifix ripped off his neck. They want a bit of your hair, a bit of your clothes....anything to say that it belongs to you. It was scary, but exciting at the same time."

But Westlife were blown away by the support they enjoyed there. "We had huge audiences coming to see our show. We never had a response like it anywhere in the world."

westlife

First published in Great Britain in 1999

1 3 5 7 9 10 8 6 4 2

Copyright © 1999 Westlife

Eddie Rowley has asserted his right to be identified as the author of this work.

All Rights Reserved. Used Under Authorisation.
Title and character and place names protected by all applicable laws.

All rights reserved. No part of this publication may be reproduced, stored in a retrieval system, or transmitted in any form
or by any means, electronic, mechanical, photocopying, recording or otherwise, without prior permission from the copyright owners

Ebury Press
Random House, 20 Vauxhall Bridge Road, London SW1V 2SA

Random House Australia Pty Limited
20 Alfred Street, Milsons Point, Sydney, New South Wales 2061, Australia

Random House New Zealand Limited
18 Poland Road, Glenfield, Auckland 10, New Zealand

Random House South Africa (Pty) Limited
Endulini, 5A Jubilee Road, Parktown 2193, South Africa

The Random House Group. Limited Reg. No. 954009

A CIP catalogue record for this book is available from the British Library

ISBN 0 09 187 423 8

All photographs supplied by Idols Licensing and Publicity Ltd

Photographers: Fryderyk Gabowicz, Martin Gardner, Tom Howard, Ulf Magnusson, Fabio Nosotti, Mike Prior

Thank you to Smash Hits and TV Hits magazines for their assistance

Designed by Blackjacks

Printed and bound in Italy by New Interlitho S.P.A.

Papers used by Ebury Press are natural, recyclable products made from wood grown in sustainable forests.

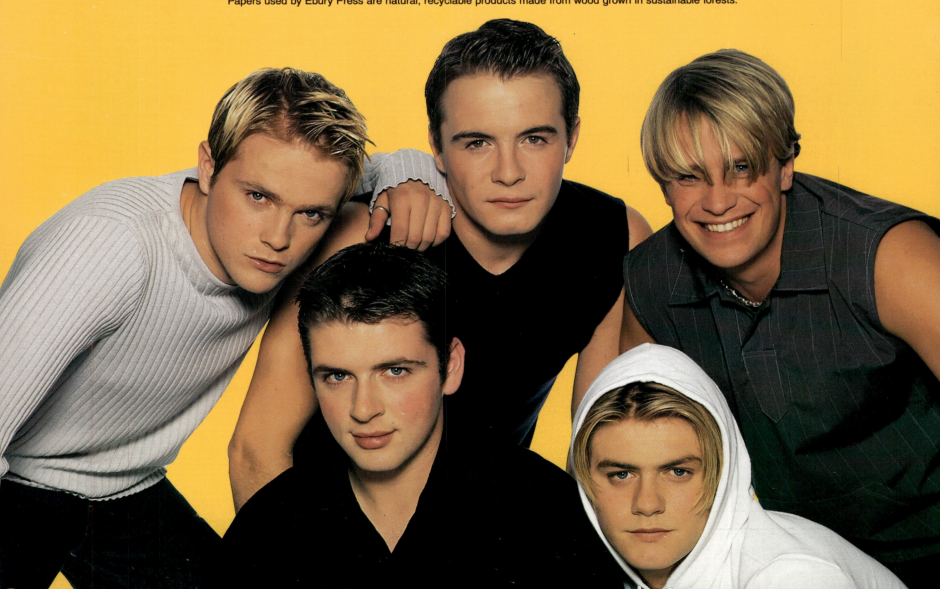